AESOP, *Five Centuries of Illustrated Fables*

ESOPVS

AESOP

Five Centuries of Illustrated Fables

Selected by John J. McKendry

The Metropolitan Museum of Art

Distributed by New York Graphic Society, Greenwich, Connecticut

FRONTISPIECE: German woodcut,
frontispiece from Aesop's Life and Fables,
Ulm, about 1476–77.

I would like to express my gratitude to my colleagues in the Museum's Department of Prints, Hyatt Mayor, Janet Byrne, Caroline Karpinski, Susanne Udell, Mary Myers, and Mary Norcott Pemberton, without whose help and patience this book would have been impossible; I would also like to thank Karl Kup, Elizabeth Roth, and Wilson Duprey of the Print Division of the New York Public Library for their assistance.

J. J. M.

Introduction

The fables of Aesop are the only text that has been illustrated so often, so diversely, and so continuously that the history of the printed illustrated book can be shown by them alone. Illustrated Bibles outnumber the fables, but the sacred text imposes a more hieratic and less varied approach. Ovid's *Metamorphoses* accounts for a great number of illustrated books, but this classical author has suffered many periods of neglect. The fables' combination of freedom of approach and constant appeal has kept them steadily popular as a subject for book illustration from the fifteenth century to the present.

Basically, the fables are didactic tales. The reader is supposed either to emulate or to beware of the behavior of the actors when faced with a similar situation. Exactly what the fables are to teach depends on the teller. Over the centuries, his attitude has ranged from worldliness — even complete cynicism — to adherence to a rigidly orthodox moral code. The stories are sometimes told with no comment, left to speak for themselves, with at most a moral vaguely implied. At other times they have had to carry the weight of long preambles, elaborate descriptions, detailed conclusions, and ponderous reflections. The same fable has even been given completely different interpretations. The fox who called the inaccessible grapes green has been considered the prototype of the man who, unable to achieve a desired end, maintains that it was not what he wanted, so much so that the expression "sour grapes" tersely conveys all there is to say about this type of self-delusion. In Caxton's translation, however, the fox is considered wise for rejecting an unattainable goal.

The fables lend themselves easily to illustration, for they are stories in which both actors and actions are simplified. The actors are sometimes humans, gods, or inanimate objects given the power of speech, but most

5

often they are animals. These animals act and talk like humans, but humans whose behavior is shorn of any complications in order to emphasize a single characteristic. There are seldom more than three characters; most often there are two. If there are others, they usually act as a single group. The action also is straightforward; there is usually one crucial act of crucial brevity, and there is rarely any great lapse of time. Conversely, although the fables are easy to illustrate, the illustrations do not explain themselves, and picture and story are bound together. Thus, the fables are best suited to book illustration; they do not easily lend themselves to treatment on the grand scale, in painting or sculpture.

The fables are not fixed firmly in a time or place, an important reason for their continuing popularity with illustrators. Each artist who treats them is free to set them in the period in which he feels most at home, or else (which is quite usual) to depict them with no specific location. There are two reasons for this: first, the simplicity of the stories specifies no circumstantial detail. Also, and very important, there is no definitive text for Aesop. None of the surviving texts purports to be Aesop's own, nor even a copy after a lost original. The earliest one, the Latin verse version by Phaedrus from the first century A.D., is, like those that followed, not a translation but a retelling of the stories.

Aesop's name is linked with the fables from the fifth century B.C. He is traditionally believed to have been a Phrygian slave who lived in the sixth century B.C. He was a hunchback, born dumb, but given the gift of speech by the goddess Isis for his devotion to her. His talent for telling fables enabled him to make fools of his masters, and he won his freedom and became the adviser of kings. But his fortune was short-lived; he was falsely accused and convicted of theft by the citizens of Delphi, and he was executed by being thrown from a cliff. The life is doubtless apocryphal; what is important is that Aesop was noted for his storytelling.

A collection of Aesopic fables in Greek prose is mentioned by Diogenes Laertius as having been made by Demetrius of Phalerum in the fourth century B.C., and the surviving later Greek manuscripts may go back to this earliest known source. There are fables that predate Aesop; some appear in Greek literature as early as Hesiod, two centuries before Aesop's presumed birth. Animals behave as humans in the art of civilizations earlier than Greece, and vestiges of fables remain from India and Asia Minor, but the

6

origins are too tenuous, too uncertain to be traced. It is certain, however, that the compilation of fables labelled Aesop's is a conglomerate one.[1] Aesop was not primarily an innovator, although, like many who retold the fables, he probably invented some. [1]

In this edition of the fables each illustration has been matched with a more or less contemporaneous translation. For some stories, the text and illustration are from the same source. The first printed edition of Aesop in English was that of Caxton, in 1484; Caxton himself had made the translation, from an earlier French version, and this seems to have been the standard, indeed the only, English version for about a century. In 1585, Bullokar, an educator and advocate of spelling reform, made a fresh translation of Aesop, which is distinctive in being written with his particular brand of spelling (which, like that of all the older translations, has been standardized in this edition). Ogilby and L'Estrange in the seventeenth century produced versions of great originality. Croxall's translation of 1722 became the standard English one for most of his century; Bewick's later replaced it with one giving even more emphasis to the moral lessons of the tales. In the nineteenth and twentieth centuries, translations of good, if not exceptional, quality proliferated. But no English writer ever equalled La Fontaine, whose retelling with new inventions gives the fables a position they have only in France, that of a major literary monument, and is the only possible telling of the fables in French.

No single illustrated edition, from any country, ever set a standard to which all other versions must be compared. There is no edition of the fables comparable to Dürer's *Apocalypse*, which makes all subsequent treatments of the theme virtually impossible. There is nothing similar to Manet's lithographs for Poe's *The Raven*, those of Delacroix for Goethe's *Faust*, Moreau le Jeune's engravings for Rousseau's *La Nouvelle Héloise*, or Tenniel's wood engravings for *Alice in Wonderland*, where writer and illustrator had a rapport that could exist only once. Nor is Aesop one of those authors, like Homer, Shakespeare, or Dante, whose words overpower any attempt to translate them into a visual equivalent, so that illustrations can only be a pale reminder of the text.

Although the fables had been illustrated from early times, the invention of the printing press produced a virtual onslaught of the illustrations and made them a major part of our pictorial history. Before the end of the

fifteenth century, there were over twenty different illustrated editions of them. The earliest editions are those of Mondovi, Ulm, and Verona, all published between 1476 and 1479, which are among the best books of the fifteenth century.

In these editions the animals are simply drawn, with a minimum of background, a tree perhaps, or a cluster of buildings if the setting is urban. The interest is in the central incident of the fable. The Mondovi Aesop, with its appealingly awkward metal cuts, dates possibly from 1476 and is usually called the earliest. It unfortunately is not in our collection (nor in any other in America), so cannot be shown here. The Ulm woodcuts are the first German book illustrations that show the hand of a distinctive personality. They were republished in Augsburg a few years later and were the most popular and most copied versions of the fifteenth century. The Verona Aesop is quite different; the cuts are rougher, as though the cutter had designed them with his knife. Another major fifteenth-century Aesop is the Naples edition of 1485. Its illustrations, surrounded with decorative borders, are particularly lively and capture the dramatic moment with a special effectiveness.

In the next century there is a greater variety of approach. The new technique of etching permits a more freely drawn line; shading and details are easier to render. There is more interest in the animals as animals, and the illustrations, particularly Geeraerts', show a keen observation of them. Landscape and background also become more elaborated.

Two English editions stand out in the seventeenth century. Barlow's illustrations, published first in 1666, are freely, almost carelessly etched and have a pleasant, unsophisticated naturalism. In complete contrast are the engravings of Hollar, the itinerant artist who came to England in the mid-seventeenth century and did much of his best work there. His very elegant engravings for the editions of 1665 and 1668 combine the most detailed observation of nature with backgrounds that often depict places he had visited. Despite the originality of most of his compositions, a number of them, including that of *The Lion and the Mouse*, are borrowed almost exactly from Geeraerts. Altogether different was the French edition of 1677, which records the labyrinth at Versailles, whose mazes were interspersed with fountains depicting the fables, alluding to their role as a guide through life. Unfortunately, except for a few pieces of sculpture, the foun-

8

tains were destroyed when fashions in gardening changed, so the *Labyrinte* is the only record of these charming and most rare three-dimensional renderings of the fables.

In the eighteenth century the outstanding edition is the deluxe La Fontaine with large engravings after Oudry. Oudry's drawings, engraved by Cochin and other excellent engravers, depict the fables within Régence settings, whose richness, in some cases, almost overwhelms the incidents. Crude in comparison to this elegant book is the design for transfer to a plate. The technique of transferring an etched or engraved design onto pottery was developed soon after the middle of the century as a cheap substitute for hand painting. Since it was impossible to transfer the design directly from the metal to the piece of pottery, an impression was taken onto a soft cloth, and then applied to the plate. The design reproduced here is in reverse, since it is a proof taken on paper before the second reversal that would correct it.

With each century the interests of the artists became more varied, just as do the techniques for illustration. In the fifteenth century simple woodcuts or metal cuts were the only possible means of reproduction, whereas by the nineteenth century etching, engraving, wood engraving, lithography, and photogravure were all available. The invention of wood engraving, in particular, multiplied editions of Aesop as never before. Bewick popularized this technique, which consists of engraving the end grain of a block of hard wood with tools similar to those used to engrave metal and printing the cut, like a woodcut, at the same time as the type. He used it late in the eighteenth century when he did his first Aesop. This and the revised editions of 1818 and 1823 are not among Bewick's best works and are on the whole surprisingly derivative considering his talent for animal illustration. He drew much from Croxall's metal cuts of 1722, which in turn were based mainly on the first illustrated La Fontaine of 1668 by Chauveau, which was itself to a great extent dependent on Barlow's and even Geeraerts' earlier illustrations. Before the middle of the century there were, however, a number of other editions using wood engraving. Grandville's illustrations of 1838 and 1839 are especially effective. He had much practice depicting humans in the guise of animals, for many of his caricatures were done in this style, and he turned easily to depicting animals behaving like humans. In Doré's edition of 1868, the animals move in a murky sinister world, very like the world of his *Inferno* illustrations, though many of the smaller vignettes are in the lighter, quite humorous vein in which he was equally at home.

Just when wood engraving had reached the peak of elaboration, the introduction of photoetching enormously simplified the reproduction of drawings. Crane's are among the earliest Aesop illustrations in this new technique. Their somewhat Art Nouveau exuberance is particularly suited to the crowded composition of *The Birds, The Beasts, and The Bat*. Both Rackham and Calder reproduced their very different but equally delightful drawings by this means.

It is fitting to close this selection with the works of two contemporary artists who have returned to techniques very similar to those used in the earliest Aesops. Frasconi's woodcuts and Low's linoleum cuts resemble the fifteenth-century Aesops in their simplicity and vitality, but they would no more be mistaken for them than the Ulm and other editions of the 1470's would be taken for twentieth-century works.

Bewick felt that the Aesop of Croxall had led hundreds of youths into the paths of wisdom and rectitude. The aim of this edition is hardly so lofty; it is simply to make its readers aware of the enormous variety and quantity of the illustrations of the fables. Whatever other effects it may have are the responsibility of Aesop.

JOHN J. McKENDRY
Assistant Curator of Prints

AESOP, *Five Centuries of Illustrated Fables*

The Fox and the Grapes

A fox looked and beheld the grapes that grew upon a huge vine, the which grapes he much desired for to eat them. And when he saw that none he might get, he turned his sorrow into joy, and said, "These grapes are sour, and if I had some I would not eat them."

He is wise which faineth not to desire the thing the which he may not have.

German woodcut from
Aesop's Life and Fables,
Ulm, about 1476–77.
Translation adapted from
William Caxton, 1484.

The Ant and the Grasshopper

A grasshopper in the wintertime went and demanded of the ant some of her corn for to eat. And then the ant said to the grasshopper, "What hast thou done all the summer last past?" And the grasshopper answered, "I have sung." And after said the ant to her, "Of my corn shalt thou none have, and if thou hast sung all the summer, dance now in winter."

There is one time for to do some labor and work, and one time for to have rest, for he that worketh not nor does no good shall have oft at his teeth great cold, and lack at his need.

German woodcut from
Aesop's Life and Fables,
Ulm, about 1476–77.
Translation adapted from
William Caxton, 1484.

The Hart, the Sheep, and the Wolf

A hart, in the presence of a wolf, demanded of a sheep that she should pay a bushel of corn, and the wolf commanded to the sheep to pay it. And when the day of payment was come, the hart came and demanded of the sheep his corn. And the sheep said to him, "The covenants and pacts made by dread and force ought not to be holding. For it was forced on me, being before the wolf, to promise and grant to give to thee that which thou never lent to me. And therefore thou shalt have right nought of me."

Sometimes it is good to make promise of something for to eschew greater damage or loss, for the things which are done by force have none fidelity.

Italian woodcut from
Aesop's Fables,
Verona, 1479.
Translation adapted from
William Caxton, 1484.

The Dog and His Shadow

In time past was a dog that went over a bridge, and held in his mouth a piece of meat, and as he passed over the bridge, he perceived and saw the shadow of himself and of his piece of meat within the water. And he, thinking that it was another piece of meat, forthwith thought to take it. And as he opened his mouth, the piece of meat fell into the water, and thus he lost it.

He that desires to have another man's good often loses his own.

Italian woodcut from
Aesop's Fables,
Verona, 1479.
Translation adapted from
William Caxton, 1484.

The Frogs Who Wanted a King

Italian woodcut from
Aesop's Life and Fables,
Naples, 1485.
Translation adapted from
William Caxton, 1484.

There were frogs which were in ditches and ponds at their liberty. They all together of one assent and of one will made a request to Jupiter that he would give them a king. And Jupiter began thereof to marvel. And for their king he cast to them a great piece of wood, which made a great sound and noise in the water, whereof all the frogs had a great dread and feared much. And after, they approached to their king for to make obeisance unto him. And when they perceived that it was but a piece of wood, they turned again to Jupiter, praying him sweetly that he would give to them another king. And Jupiter gave to them the heron for to be their king. And then the heron began to enter into the water and eat them one after another. And when the frogs saw that their king destroyed and ate them thus, they began tenderly to weep, saying in this manner to the god Jupiter, "Right high and right mighty god Jupiter, please thee to deliver us from the throat of this dragon and false tyrant which eateth us the one after another." And he said to them, "The king which you have demanded shall be your master. For when men have that which men ought to have, they ought to be joyful and glad. And he that has liberty ought to keep it well, for nothing is better than liberty."

Liberty should not be well sold for all the gold and silver of all the world.

The Lion and the Horse

A lion saw a horse which ate grass in a meadow. And to find some subtlety and manner to eat and devour him, approached to him and said, "God keep thee, my brother. I am a leech and withal a good physician. And because I see that thou hast a sore foot, I am come hither for to heal thee of it." And the horse knew well all his evil thought, and said to the lion, "My brother, I thank thee greatly, and thou art welcome to me. I pray thee that thou wilt make my foot whole." And then the lion said to the horse, "Let me see thy foot." And as the lion looked on it, the horse smote him on the forehead in such wise that he broke his head and went full out of his mind and fell to the ground, and so wondrously was he hurt that almost he might not rise up again. And then said the lion in himself, "I am well worthy to have had this, for he that searcheth evil, evil cometh to him."

None ought to feign himself other than such as he is.

Italian woodcut from
Aesop's Life and Fables,
Naples, 1485.
Translation adapted from
William Caxton, 1484.

The Rat, the Frog, and the Kite

As a rat went in pilgrimage, he came by a river, and demanded help of a frog for to pass and go over the water. And then the frog bound the rat's foot to her foot, and thus swam unto the middle of the river. And as they were there the frog stood still, to the end that the rat should be drowned. And in the meanwhile came a kite upon them and bare them both with him.

He that thinketh evil against good, the evil that he thinketh shall fall upon himself.

Italian woodcut from
Aesopo Historiado,
Venice, 1497.
Translation adapted from
William Caxton, 1484.

The Frog and the Ox

A frog was in a meadow when she espied and saw an ox which pastured. She would make herself as great and as mighty as the ox, and by her great pride she began to swell against the ox, and demanded of her children if she was not as great as the ox and as mighty. And her children answered and said, "Nay Mother, for to look and behold on the ox it seemeth of you to be nothing." And then the frog began more to swell. And when the ox saw her pride, he trod and threshed her with his foot, and broke her belly.

Swell not thyself to the end that thou break not.

Italian woodcut from
Aesopo Historiado,
Venice, 1497.
Translation adapted from
William Caxton, 1484.

The Ass and the Boar

While the dull ass the sturdy boar derides,
The boar, whose passion sounder reason guides,
Replies, "Dull villain, that the world may see
How much I slight thy scoffs, although from me
Thou just revenge deservst, jest on thy fill,
Thy baseness guards thee, and withholds my will."

Do not enraged at all aspersions grow
Lest false untruths like verities may show.

Woodcut after Titian (?)
from *Cento Favole Morali*,
Venice, 1577.
Translation by
William Barret, 1639.

The Wolf and the Lamb

A thirsty lamb walks to the river's side,
Where she is by a ravenous wolf espied,
Whose currish nature (still on mischief bent)
Thus picks a quarrel with the innocent
And harmless beast: "What villain moved thee thus
Just in our presence (as in scorn of us)
Ere we could drink, to foul the crystal spring?"
The lamb, affrighted at his menacing,
Replied, "Great sir, the cause of my offense
Was through my ignorance, not insolence;
Nor did I know, that you were present here;"
At which the wolf 'gins more to domineer,
And answers, "Slave thou liest; have not I seen
How ready thou, and all thy friends have been,
To cross us still? for which (without delay)
Thy blood for all those former wrongs shall pay."

So great men often times o'ersway with might
The poor, against respect of law or right.

Woodcut after Titian (?)
from *Cento Favole Morali*,
Venice, 1577.
Translation by
William Barret, 1639.

The Eagle and the Fox

An eagle and a fox, a pact to dwell in friendship having been made between them, thought the friendship would be the surer for being often together. Therefore the eagle began her nest upon a high tree, and the fox placed her cubs among the bushes near the tree. One day when the fox was gone out of her den to seek food for her cubs, the eagle, finding herself lacking meat, flew to the den of the fox, snatched up the fox's cubs, and gave them to her young ones to eat. The fox, returning and discovering her children's cruel death, was made very sorrowful. When she could not be revenged on the eagle, because being a four-footed beast she could not follow after a bird, she cursed the eagle and wished him evil, and the broken friendship turned into a great hatred. In those days goats were sacrificed, and the eagle snatched up a piece of one, together with burning coals, and carried it to her nest. The wind was blowing somewhat earnestly, and the nest, which was made of hay and of small and dry stuff, was set on fire. The eagle's young ones, feeling the flame, fell down on the ground, for they could not fly as yet. The fox, snatching them up, straightway devoured them in the eagle's sight.

They that violate friendship, although they get away from the revenge of those whom they hurt, yet do not escape punishment.

Italian etching from
Fabulae Centum, Rome, 1565.
Translation adapted from
William Bullokar, 1585.

The Fly

A fly that had fallen into a pot of meat, perceiving that she should be stifled in the brine, sayeth with her own self, "Lo, I have drunk so much, I have eaten so much, I have washed me so much, that I may rightfully die, being full fed."

It is the point of a wise man to bear with a mighty courage that thing that can in no wise be avoided.

Italian etching from
Fabulae Centum, Rome, 1565.
Translation adapted from
William Bullokar, 1585.

i 4

The Fox and the Goat

A fox and a goat being very thirsty went down into a well, wherein, when they had thoroughly drunk, the fox sayeth to the goat, looking about for the way back again: "O goat, be of good courage, for I have devised by what means both may be at liberty again. If thou wilt lift thyself upright, thy forefeet being moved to the wall, and shalt bend up thy horns, thy chin being brought to thy breast, then I, leaping over by thy back and horns, and going away out of the well, will guide thee out then afterward." To which council the goat had trust, and obeyed as she bid, and the fox leapt out of the well, and afterward for joy capered on the brim of the well and rejoiced greatly, having no care of the goat. But when she was accused by the goat as a breaker of promises, she answered: "Truly O goat, if thou hadst as much perceiving in thy mind as thou hast long hairs on thy chin, thou wouldst not have gone down into the well before thou hadst had assurance of returning."

A wise man ought to search the end before he comes to do a thing through.

Etching by Marcus Geeraerts
from *De Warachtighe Fabulen
der Dieren*, Bruges, 1567.
Translation adapted from
William Bullokar, 1585.

The Hares and the Frogs

A wood making noise with an unaccustomed threatening wind, the hares, being fearful, ran away with all speed. When there stood a post against them running away, they stood doubtfully, being compassed with dangers on both sides. And because there might be a provoking of greater fear, they saw frogs too who dived in a brook. The one of the hares being skillfuller and wiser than the rest sayeth, "Why do we fear in vain? We have need of courage. Truly we have nimbleness of body, but we lack stomach. This danger of the blustering wind is not to be fled, but it is to be set right by."

Men have need of courage in every thing. Virtue lyeth down without boldness, for steadfast trust is the guide and queen of virtue.

Etching by Marcus Geeraerts
from *De Warachtighe Fabulen der Dieren*, Bruges, 1567.
Translation adapted from
William Bullokar, 1585.

The Two Crabs

Between two crabs, the mother and the son,
A conference held; the mother thus begun
To check her young one, that he did not go
A comely pace, but waddled to and fro;
To whom the son replied, "Mother, I pray,
Mind your gait first, and I shall find the way."

First set thyself upright, and then
Thou boldly mayest check other men.

Engraving by
Wenceslaus Hollar for
Aesopics, London, 1668.
Translation by
William Barret, 1639.

The Lion and the Mouse

Upon the roaring of a beast in the wood, a mouse ran presently out to see what news: and what was it, but a lion hampered in a net! This accident brought to her mind, how that she herself, but some few days before, had fallen under the paw of a certain generous lion, that let her go again. Upon a strict enquiry into the matter, she found this to be that very lion; and so set herself presently to work upon the couplings of the net; gnawed the threads to pieces, and in gratitude delivered her preserver.

Without good nature, and gratitude, men had as good live in a wilderness as in a society. There is no subject so inconsiderable, but his prince, at some time or other, may have occasion for him, and it holds through the whole scale of the creation, that the great and the little have need one of another.

Engraving by
Wenceslaus Hollar for
The Fables of Aesop,
London, 1665.
Translation by
Sir Roger L'Estrange, 1692.

42

W. Hollar fecit

The Fox and the Crane

The fox the crane did solemnly invite
Only to tantalize her appetite,
For nothing he but liquid fare provides
That spreading o'er the table thinly glides,
Of which her spearlike beak could nothing sup,
Whilst the sly fox licks all unkindly up.
The crane, this false imposture to requite
The fox to new carresses did invite,
But a glass vial did her cates contain,
Which only she with length of bill could drain.
The fox, thus foiled with her more powerful arts,
To his own cell with scorn and shame departs.

Thus fraud t'entangle fraud is oft designed,
And falsehood is by falsehood countermined.

Etching after Francis Barlow from
Aesop's Fables with His Life,
London, 1687.
Translation by
Thomas Philipott, 1666.

The Dog and the Ox

The envious dog that brooding lay,
Upon a crib replete with hay,
Snarls at the ox that thither came,
An eager appetite to tame.
And forced him back, incensed, whereat
He on the dog invokes this fate:
May the just gods so punish thee
As thy rude spleen hath injured me
Who does prohibit me the meat
Whereon thyself disdains to eat.

Some with keen envy would themselves annoy,
So those they emulate they might destroy.

Etching after Francis Barlow from
Aesop's Fables with His Life,
London, 1687.
Translation by
Thomas Philipott, 1666.

The Fox and the Carved Head

As a fox was rummaging among a great many carved figures, there was one very extraordinary piece among the rest. He took it up, and when he had considered it a while, "Well," says he, "what pity 'tis, that so exquisite an outside of a head should not have one grain of sense in't."

'Tis not the barber or the tailor that makes the man, and 'tis no new thing to see a fine wrought head without so much as one grain of salt in't.

Etching by
Sébastien Leclerc from
Labyrinte de Versailles,
Paris, 1677.
Translation by
Sir Roger L'Estrange, 1692.

Le Clerc.

The Swan and the Stork

A stork that was present at the song of a dying swan told her 'twas contrary to nature to sing so much out of season, and asked her the reason of it. "Why," says the swan, "I am now entering into a state where I shall be no longer in danger of either snares, guns, or hunger: and who would not joy at such a deliverance?"

Death is but a last farewell to all the difficulties, pains, and hazards of life.

Etching by
Sébastien Leclerc from
Labyrinte de Versailles,
Paris, 1677.
Translation by
Sir Roger L'Estrange, 1692.

The Lioness and the Fox

Metal cut attributed to
Elisha Kirkall, and
translation by Samuel Croxall
from *Fables of Aesop
and Others*, London, 1722.

A lioness and a fox, chancing to meet together, fell into discourse; and the conversation turning upon the breeding, and the fruitfulness, of some living creatures above others, the fox could not forbear taking the opportunity of observing to the lioness, that for her part she thought foxes were as happy in that respect as almost any other creatures; for that they bred constantly once a year, if not oftener, and always had a good litter of cubs at every birth. "And yet," says she, "there are those, who are never delivered of more than one at a time, and that perhaps not above once or twice through their whole life, who hold up their noses and value themselves so much upon it, that they think all other creatures beneath them, and scarce worthy to be spoken to." The lioness, who all the while perceived at whom this reflection pointed, colored with resentment, and, with a good deal of vehemence, replied, "Mrs. Fox, what you have observed is certainly true, and, if you don't know, I'll give you reason why it ought to be so. You produce a great many at a litter, and often: but what are they? Foxes. I indeed have but one at a time, but remember that this one is a lion; a lion, Mrs. Fox."

Production is not to be esteemed so much by quantity as by quality.

The Viper and the File

A viper, seizing on a hardened file,
Gnawed the rough tool, that did her hopes beguile
And, in derision, cried, "Vain fool, forbear;
Thy teeth thou may'st, but me thou canst not wear:
I that on brass and steel am daily fed,
From thy soft grinders no impression dread."

Be always cautious whom thou dost engage,
Lest thou repent thy insuccessful rage:
He who encounters with too potent foes,
Misspends his anger, and himself undoes.

Engraving after
Jean Baptiste Oudry from
Fables Choisies,
Paris, 1755–59.
Translation by
Edmund Arwaker, 1708.

The Town Mouse and the Country Mouse

A contented country mouse had once the honor to receive a visit from an old acquaintance belonging to the court. The country mouse, extremely glad to see her guest, very hospitably set before her the best cheese and bacon which her cottage afforded; and as to their beverage, it was the purest water from the spring. The repast was homely indeed, but the welcome hearty: they sat and chatted away the evening together very agreeably, and then retired in peace and quietness each to her little cell. The next morning when the guest was to take her leave, she kindly pressed her country friend to accompany her; setting forth in very pompous terms, the great elegance and plenty in which she lived at court. The country mouse was easily prevailed upon, and they set out together. It was late in the evening when they arrived at the palace; however, in one of the rooms, they found the remains of a sumptuous entertainment. There were creams and jellies, and sweetmeats; and everything, in short, of the most delicate kind: the cheese was Parmesan, and they wetted their whiskers in exquisite champagne. But before they had half finished their repast, they were alarmed with the barking and scratching of a lap dog; then the mewing of a cat frightened them almost to death; by and by, a whole train of servants burst into the room, and everything was swept away in an instant. "Ah! my dear friend," said the country mouse, as soon as she had recovered courage enough to speak, "if your fine living is thus interrupted with fears and dangers, let me return to my plain food, and my peaceful cottage; for what is elegance without ease; or plenty, with an aching heart?"

Engraving after
Jean Baptiste Oudry from
Fables Choisies,
Paris, 1755–59.
Translation by
Robert Dodsley, 1764.

The Wolves and the Sheep

French etching for
transfer to plate, about 1800.
Translation by
Robert Thomson, 1806.

After a thousand years of war declared,
The sheep and wolves on peace agreed,
Of which it seems both parties stood in need;
For if the wolves no fleecy wanderer spared,
The angry shepherds hunted them the more,
And skins of wolves for coats in triumph wore.
No freedom either knew,
The harmless sheep or bloody crew;
Trembling they ate, or from their food were driven,
Till peace was made, and hostages were given.
The sheep gave up their dogs, the wolves their young.
Exchange was made, and signed and sealed
By commissaries on the field.
Our little wolves soon after getting strong,
Nay, wolves complete, and longing now to kill,
The shepherds' absence watched with care.
One day, when all within the fold was still,
They worried half the lambs, the fattest there,
And in their teeth into the forest bore.
Their tribes they slyly had informed before.
The dogs, who thought the treaty sure,
Were worried as they slept secure;
So quick that none had time to wail,
For none escaped to tell the tale.

From hence we may conclude —
That war with villains never ought to end.
Peace in itself, I grant, is good,
But what is peace with savages so rude,
Who scoff at faith and stab a peaceful friend?

58

LES LOUPS ET LES BREBIS.

The Crow and the Pitcher

A crow, ready to die with thirst, flew with joy to a pitcher which he beheld at some distance. When he came, he found water in it indeed, but so near the bottom, that with all his stooping and straining, he was not able to reach it. Then he endeavored to overturn the pitcher, that so at least he might be able to get a little of it; but his strength was not sufficient for this. At last, seeing some pebbles lie near the place, he cast them one by one into the pitcher; and thus, by degrees, raised the water up to the very brim, and satisfied his thirst.

What we cannot compass by force, we may by invention and industry.

When frowning fates thy sanguine hopes defeat,
And virtuous aims with disappointment meet,
Submit not to despair, th' attempt renew,
And rise superior to the vulgar crew.

Wood engraving and translation
by Thomas Bewick for
*Select Fables of Aesop and
Others*, Newcastle, 1784.

The Stag and His Antlers

That good from bad men rarely know
This apologue may serve to show:
A stag upon a fountain's side,
Beheld his branching horns with pride;
While of his spindle-shanks ashamed,
Their disproportioned form he blamed.
Sudden he hears the hunter's cries,
And to the forest nimbly flies.
The woods receive their well-known guest;
His tangled horns his feet arrest;
The hounds approach, and seize their prey,
Who, dying, thus was heard to say:
"Wretch that I am! too late I learn,
How little we the truth discern!
What would have saved me I despised,
And what has been my ruin, prized!"

Etching by Samuel Howitt
from *A New Work of Animals*,
London, 1811.
Translation by
Sir Brooke Boothby, 1809.

The Fox without a Tail

A sly old fox, a foe of geese and rabbits,
Was taken captive in a trap one day
(Just recompense of predatory habits),
And lost his tail before he got away.
He felt ashamed at such a mutilation;
But, cunning as before, proposed a way
To gain companions in his degradation;
And spoke as follows, on a council-day:
"Dear brother foxes, what can be the beauty
Or use of things so cumbrous and absurd?
They only sweep the mud up. It's your duty
To cut them off — it is, upon my word!"
"Not bad advice: there *may* be wisdom in it,"
Remarked a sage, "but will you, by-the-by,
Oblige us all by turning round a minute,
Before we give a positive reply?"
You never heard such hurricanes of laughter
As hailed the cropped appearance of the rogue,
Of course, among the foxes, ever after,
Long tails continued very much in vogue.

Engraving by G. Gouget
from *Fables de La Fontaine*,
Paris, 1833–34.
Translation by
Walter Thornbury, after 1868.

The Ape and the Dolphin

Your good sense by your silence would better be shown,
Than pretending to know what is really unknown;
The Greek sailors were wont apes and puppies to keep,
To amuse the dull time that they passed on board ship.
When off Sunium, a galley that carried an ape
Was o'erset in a storm, and all tossed in the deep.
As it happened near Athens, the passengers strain
Every effort by swimming the city to gain;
Next the ape chanced a dolphin to swim by good luck,
When the fish took him up for a man on his back;
As his charge through the port of Piraeus he bore,
He demanded of him whether born on the shore;
"An Athenian, I am," cried the ape, "and well bred."
"Then no doubt our Piraeus you know," the fish said.
"My good friend is Piraeus," the monkey rejoined,
"Never lived a companion more pleasant nor kind."
"O ho, friend!" said the dolphin, "I find you're a knave,"
Then dived down with his burden at once in the wave.

Engraving by G. Gouget
from *Fables de La Fontaine*,
Paris, 1833–34.
Translation by
J. F. Byrne, 1835.

The Sick Stag

A stag, where stags abounded,
Fell sick, and was surrounded
Forthwith by comrades kind,
All pressing to assist,
Or see, their friend, at least,
And ease his anxious mind —
An irksome multitude.
"Ah, sirs!" the sick was fain to cry,
"Pray leave me here to die,
As others do, in solitude.
Pray, let your kind attentions cease,
Till death my spirit shall release."
But comforters are not so sent:
On duty sad full long intent,
When Heaven pleased, they went,
But not without a friendly glass;
That is to say, they cropped the grass
And leaves which in that quarter grew,
From which the sick his pittance drew.
By kindness thus compelled to fast,
He died for want of food at last.

The men take off no trifling dole
Who heal the body or the soul.
Alas the times! do what we will,
They have their payment, cure or kill.

Wood engraving after
J. J. Grandville from
Fables de La Fontaine,
Paris, 1838.
Translation by
Elizur Wright, Jr., 1841.

The Hare and the Tortoise

A hare jeered at a tortoise for the slowness of his pace. But he laughed and said, that he would run against her and beat her any day she should name. "Come on," said the hare, "you shall soon see what my feet are made of." So it was agreed that they should start at once. The tortoise went off jogging along, without a moment's stopping, at his usual steady pace. The hare, treating the whole matter very lightly, said she would first take a little nap, and that she should soon overtake the tortoise. Meanwhile the tortoise plodded on, and the hare oversleeping herself, arrived at the goal, only to see that the tortoise had got in before her.

Slow and steady wins the race.

Wood engraving after
J. J. Grandville
from *Fables de La Fontaine*,
Paris, 1838.
Translation by
Thomas James, 1848.

70

The Mice in Council

Once upon a time, the mice, being sadly distressed by the persecution of the cat, resolved to call a meeting, to decide upon the best means of getting rid of this continual annoyance. Many plans were discussed and rejected; at last a young mouse got up and proposed that a bell should be hung round the cat's neck, that they might for the future always have notice of her coming, and so be able to escape. This proposition was hailed with the greatest applause, and was agreed to at once unanimously. Upon which an old mouse, who had sat silent all the while, got up and said that he considered the contrivance most ingenious, and that it would, no doubt, be quite successful; but he had only one short question to put, namely, which of them it was who would bell the cat?

It is one thing to propose, and another to execute.

Wood engraving after
Gustave Doré from
The Fables of La Fontaine,
London and New York,
after 1868.
Translation by
Thomas James, 1848.

The Wolf in Shepherd's Clothing

Wood engraving after Gustave
Doré for *Fables de La Fontaine*,
Paris, 1868.
Translation by
Elizur Wright, Jr., 1841.

A wolf, whose gettings from the flocks
Began to be but few,
Bethought himself to play the fox
In character quite new.
A shepherd's hat and coat he took,
A cudgel for a crook,
Nor e'en the pipe forgot
And more, to seem what he was not,
Himself upon his hat he wrote,
I'm Willie, shepherd of these sheep.
His person thus complete,
His crook in upraised feet,
The impostor Willie stole upon the keep.
The real Willie, on the grass asleep,
Slept there, indeed, profoundly,
His dog and pipe slept, also, soundly;
His drowsy sheep around lay,
As for the greatest number.
Much blessed the hypocrite their slumber,
And hoped to drive away the flock,
Could he the shepherd's voice but mock.
He thought undoubtedly he could.
He tried; the tone in which he spoke,
Loud echoing from the wood,
The plot and slumber broke;

74

Sheep, dog, and man awoke.
The wolf, in sorry plight,
In hampering coat bedight,
Could neither run nor fight.

There's always leakage of deceit
Which makes it never safe to cheat.
Whoever is a wolf had better
Keep clear of hypocritic fetter.

The Birds, the Beasts, and the Bat

The birds were at war with the beasts, and many battles were fought with varying success on either side. The bat did not throw in his lot definitely with either party, but when things went well for the birds he was found fighting in their ranks; when, on the other hand, the beasts got the upper hand, he was to be found among the beasts. No one paid any attention to him while the war lasted; but when it was over, and peace was restored, neither the birds nor the beasts would have anything to do with so double-faced a traitor, and so he remains to this day a solitary outcast from both.

Drawing by Walter Crane
for *The Baby's Own Aesop*,
London and New York, 1886.
Translation by
V. S. Vernon Jones, 1916.

:NEITHER·BEAST·NOR·BIRD:

Beast he
would be, or
a bird,
As might suit, thought the Bat:
but he erred.
When the battle was done,
He found that no one
Would take him for friend at
his word.

·BETWEEN·TWO·STOOLS·
·YOU·MAY·COME·TO·THE·GROUND·

The Owl and the Birds

The owl is a very wise bird; and once, long ago, when the first oak sprouted in the forest, she called all the other birds together and said to them, "You see this tiny tree? If you take my advice, you will destroy it now when it is small: for when it grows big, the mistletoe will appear upon it, from which birdlime will be prepared for your destruction." Again, when the first flax was sown, she said to them, "Go and eat up that seed, for it is the seed of the flax, out of which men will one day make nets to catch you." Once more, when she saw the first archer, she warned the birds that he was their deadly enemy, who would wing his arrows with their own feathers and shoot them. But they took no notice of what she said: in fact, they thought she was rather mad, and laughed at her. When, however, everything turned out as she had foretold, they changed their minds and conceived a great respect for her wisdom. Hence, whenever she appears, the birds attend upon her in the hope of hearing something that may be for their good. She, however, gives them advice no longer, but sits moping and pondering on the folly of her kind.

Drawing by Arthur Rackham
and translation by V. S. Vernon
Jones from *Aesop's Fables*,
London and New York, 1916.

The Fox and the Crow

On his airy perch among the branches
Master Crow was holding cheese in his beak.
Master Fox, whose pose suggested fragrances,
Said in language which of course I cannot speak,
"Aha, superb Sir Ebony, well met.
How black! Who else boasts your metallic jet!
If your warbling were unique,
Rest assured, as you are sleek,
One would say that our wood had hatched nightingales."
All aglow, Master Crow tried to run a few scales,
Risking trills and intervals,
Dropping the prize as his huge beak sang false.
The fox pounced on the cheese and remarked, "My dear sir,
Learn that every flatterer
Lives at the flattered listener's cost:
A lesson worth more than the cheese that you lost."
The tardy learner, smarting under ridicule,
Swore he'd learned his last lesson as somebody's fool.

Woodcut by Antonio Frasconi
from broadside
9 Aesop Fables, 1953.
Translation by
Marianne Moore, 1952.

The Jay in Peacock's Feathers

A jay found plumes which a moulting peacock had strewed,
Assumptively feathered himself out —
Rejoicing to parade up and down as peacocks strode about,
In what seemed an exalted mood.
Someone recognized him, and he saw the bird laugh,
Was scorned, hissed, mocked, amid all kinds of chaff,
And their lordships the peacocks plucked off his feigned coat.
Even on taking refuge with jays when the game was too rough,
The door was the reception he got.

There are plenty of ten-toed jays swaggering comically,
Purporting to be something which they cannot be.
If terms like plagiarist alarm,
Why say more? I am not one to speak dictatorially
Or do another author harm.

Woodcut by Antonio Frasconi
from broadside
9 Aesop Fables, 1953.
Translation by
Marianne Moore, 1954.

The Lion in Love

Once when a lion of high degree
Was passing through a meadowy
Place and saw a shepherdess
Whom he was avid to possess,
He went at once to ask her father.
That good man balked: for he would rather
Have had his pretty daughter marry
Someone less scary.
Afraid to bring things to a head
By ousting him, the father said:
"My daughter is delicately fashioned.
As soon as you become impassioned
You'd likely wound her with your claws.
So kindly have on all four paws
The talons trimmed. One other issue.
If this young girl is going to kiss you
With any ardor, she must be
Freed of all anxiety.
So for your own enjoyment, while
You're at it, let them file
Your teeth." The lion, love-demented,
Consented.
Behold him now without his teeth,
Without his claws, an empty sheath!
With all his native weapons gone
The helpless lion was set upon
By hounds that easily outmatched him.
They dispatched him.

Ah love, whoever bows to you
Should bid his sanity adieu!

Linoleum cut by Joseph Low,
detail, from *Aesop: a portfolio
of color prints*, Newtown, 1963.
Translation abridged from
Eunice Clark, 1948.

The Cock and the Pearl

A scratching cock struck back
A pearl, which he took
With a cluck to a jeweler,
Saying, "Exceptional —
But no grain is too small
To be treasure that I would prefer."

A blockhead was bequeathed a book
In manuscript, which he took
To a nearby connoisseur,
Remarking, "A rarity —
But a mere ha'penny
Would afford me what I would prefer."

Linoleum cut by Joseph Low,
detail, from *Aesop: a portfolio
of color prints*, Newtown, 1963.
Translation by
Marianne Moore, 1954.

Illustrations

All the illustrations are the same size as the originals, unless otherwise noted.

Translations